Working Memory Rating Scale

Manual

Tracy Packiam Alloway
Susan E. Gathercole
Hannah J. Kirkwood

PEARSON

www.pearsonclinical.co.uk

Published by Pearson Assessment, 80 Strand, London WC2R 0RL

Printed in the United Kingdom

ISBN 978 0 749151 01 0

14 15 F G

Visit our website at www.pearsonclinical.co.uk

Contents

Contents

Acknowledgements

We would like to extend our gratitude to Professor Julian Elliott for helpful discussions. We are also grateful to all the schools that participated in gathering the norms for this test. The headteachers, special needs coordinators and teachers were incredibly helpful and gave generously of their time to help us. A full list of participating schools is provided in Appendix B.

The research that provided the foundation for the *Working Memory Rating Scale* (WMRS) was supported by grants to the authors by the Medical Research Council, Economic and Social Research Council, and the British Academy.

We would also like to acknowledge the support from Pearson Assessment in the later stages of preparing the WMRS for publication, and in particular Faye Henchy for her support and guidance.

About the authors

Tracy Packiam Alloway, PhD, is a senior research psychologist based at Durham University. She is interested in how working memory affects learning and has conducted several large-scale government-funded studies on primary-aged children to find out why children with working memory impairments often fail in classroom activities. She is also involved in several projects to understand how memory affects learning in children with developmental disorders such as Attention Deficit Hyperactivity Disorder (ADHD), Autistic Spectrum Disorder (ASD), Developmental Coordination Disorder (dyspraxia), and dyscalculia (mathematical difficulties). She works closely with educational professionals and is the author of numerous academic articles and books on how children learn. The *Automated Working Memory Assessment* (AWMA) has been translated into over 10 languages, including Spanish, Italian, Dutch, Portuguese and Mandarin.

Susan E. Gathercole is a Professor of Psychology at the University of York. She is a cognitive psychologist who has been working in the area of memory and learning, particularly in children, for over 20 years, publishing approximately 100 journal articles and several books in this field. Susan is also a co-author of the *Children's Test of Nonword Repetition*, the *Reading Decision Test*, and the *Working Memory Test Battery for Children*. Her current research projects focus on both understanding and helping through classroom support and training children with a variety of developmental problems, including working memory and attentional disorders.

Hannah J. Kirkwood is an experienced primary school teacher in Durham local authority. She has taught a variety of age groups, working with pupils with a vast spectrum of individual needs from more able, gifted and talented pupils to those with severe learning, emotional and behavioural difficulties. She has also made a direct impact on the development of subject areas in schools, particularly in her role as gifted and talented coordinator. Hannah spent two years working as a research associate at York University on a project to implement and evaluate a working memory intervention programme in primary schools. She has written several case studies based on classroom observations and has contributed to journal articles based on the project.

Other tests published by the authors

Tracy Packiam Alloway
Automated Working Memory Assessment (2007). London:
Pearson Assessment

Susan E. Gathercole
Children's Test of Nonword Repetition (1996). London:
Pearson Assessment
Reading Decision Test (2005). Hove: Psychology Press
Working Memory Test Battery for Children (2001). London:
Pearson Assessment

List of equipment

The *Working Memory Rating Scale* (WMRS) consists of the following equipment:

Manual
Record Forms (x25)

Chapter 1: Introduction

The *Working Memory Rating Scale* (WMRS) is a behavioural rating scale developed for educators to facilitate easy identification of children with working memory deficits. Currently, teachers rarely identify memory as a source of difficulty in children with working memory problems, despite their poor classroom functioning. Instead, children with memory problems are typically described as inattentive. The WMRS will increase the chances of the detection and subsequent effective support in school for children with deficits of working memory.

The WMRS was developed on the basis of interviews with educators and consists of 20 items. It provides a quick and efficient way for early identification of working memory problems that will impair learning. It is suitable for ages 5 to 11. It has also been validated with the *Automated Working Memory Assessment* (AWMA) to provide a reliable tool for routine screening of memory difficulties.

Working memory: an introduction

Working memory is the term used by psychologists to refer to the ability we have to hold and manipulate information in the mind over short periods of time. It is a kind of mental workspace or jotting pad that is used to store important information in the course of our everyday lives.

One example of an activity that uses working memory is mental arithmetic. Imagine, for example, that you are attempting to multiply together the numbers *43* and *67*, in a situation where you are unable to use either a calculator or a pen and paper. To do this, you would first need to store the two numbers in working memory. The next step would be to use the multiplication rules you have already learned to calculate the products of successive pairs of numbers, adding to working memory the products as you go. Finally, you would need to add together the products held in working memory, arriving at a final solution.

This process imposes quite considerable burdens on working memory: several number combinations need to be kept in working memory for the amount of time it takes to make these calculations, and the contents of working memory have to be updated to include our number calculations as we proceed through the stages of the calculation. Without working memory, we would not be able to carry out this kind of complex mental activity without having some means to make an external record of the numbers and the calculations.

We usually experience mental activities that place significant demands on working memory as a kind of mental juggling in which we try to keep all elements of the task – in the case of mental arithmetic, the original numbers we are trying to multiply as well as the calculations we make as we proceed – going at the same time. Often, the juggling attempt will fail, either because the capacity of working memory is exceeded, or because we become distracted and our attention is diverted away from the task in hand. A minor distraction such as an unrelated thought springing to mind or an interruption by someone else is likely to result in complete loss of the stored information, and so in a failed calculation attempt. As no amount of effort will allow us to recall the lost information, the only course of action is to start the calculation afresh.

It is important to note that working memory is different from short-term memory. Psychologists use the term 'short-term memory' to refer to those situations in which the individual simply has to store some material without either mentally manipulating it in some way or doing something else at the same time. Remembering a telephone number is therefore a good example of an activity that depends on short-term memory.

Examples of commonplace activities that depend on working memory include:
- following directions such as 'When you pass the church on the left, turn immediately right and then take the second left'
- hearing an unfamiliar word in a foreign language and attempting to repeat it several seconds later
- adding up and remembering the total amount spent as you select items from shelves at the supermarket and add them to your basket
- when cooking, measuring and combining the correct amounts of ingredients (*rub in 50g of margarine and 100g of flour, then add 75g of sugar*), when you have just read the recipe but it is no longer in view
- remembering that you need to weigh 100g of flour while completing a previous step from a recipe.

Working memory in childhood

Working memory capacity steadily increases across the childhood years. The youngest age at which working memory can reliably be tested is about 4 years. The way in which working memory capacity develops with age is illustrated in Figure 1.1, which shows performance averaged across three verbal working memory tasks. The growth functions are very similar for all three aspects of working memory, with a marked increase in working memory capacity between 5 and 11 years of age, followed by small but significant increases up to 15 years, when adult levels are reached. Typically, the memory span of adults is between two and three times greater than that of young children. It is important to note that children who start off with low working memory capacity do not catch up with their peers over time, and are likely to continue to have poor working memory by the time that they become young adults. Thus, far from the working memory differences between children disappearing in later childhood, the gap between performance for the average and low working memory children actually increases with age.

Figure 1.1. *The developmental growth of working memory in childhood*

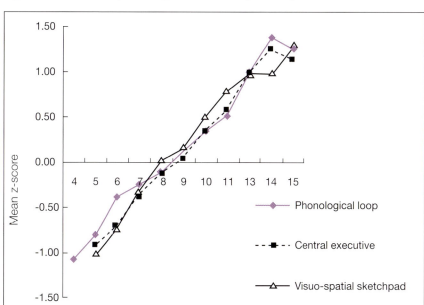

Performance on working memory tasks is subject to large degrees of individual variation. This is illustrated in Figure 1.2, which presents data from the listening recall test on the AWMA. The standardisation sample consisted of 709 children attending state primary schools in the north-east of England, aged between 4 and 11 years. *Z*-scores, which represent how each score compares to the average performance, were calculated using the trials correct measure of each test from all participating children; a score of 0 represents average performance on that measure across the entire age range. There was a steady developmental improvement in performance between 4 and 11 years. It is important to note the substantial degree of variability at each age, as reflected in the distance between the 10th and 90th centile bars for each measure. At 6.5 years, for example, the 10th centile is close to the mean for the 4.5-year-old sample, and the 90th centile approximates to the mean performance level for 9.5-year-old children. Thus, within an average class of 30 children, we would expect to see working memory capacity differences corresponding to five years of normal development between the three highest and three lowest scoring individuals. This magnitude of difference in the working memory capacities of individual children will have significant consequences for the way in which they can meet the working memory demands of classroom learning activities.

Figure 1.2. *Individual differences in working memory capacity in childhood*

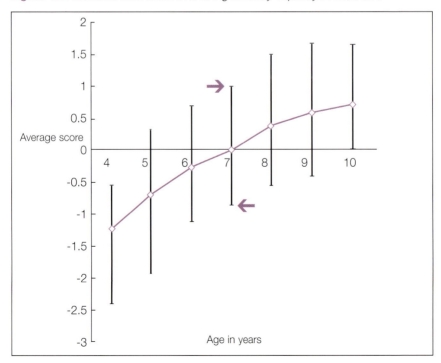

Working memory and learning

Working memory skills are closely associated with key areas of learning, such as reading and mathematics. For example, verbal working memory skills predict reading skills, and children with reading disabilities show marked working memory impairments. One explanation for the relationship between working memory and reading is that it may take considerable working memory capacity to keep in mind the relevant speech sounds and concepts necessary for successfully identifying words and comprehending text.

There is also a close relationship between verbal working memory and mathematical skills, particularly when children are learning arithmetic facts and how to retain relevant data such as carried digits. Visuospatial memory is also closely linked with mathematical skills. Visuospatial memory functions as a mental blackboard, supporting number representation, such as place value and alignment in columns, in counting and arithmetic. In young children, visuospatial memory skills are associated with performance in nonverbal problems, such as sums presented with blocks.

A key question regarding the relationship between working memory and learning disabilities is whether working memory is simply a proxy for IQ. There is evidence that working memory tasks measure something different from general intelligence tests. While IQ tests measure knowledge that the child has already learned, working memory tasks are a pure measure of a child's learning potential. Thus, working memory skills are able to predict a child's performance in both literacy and numeracy, even after a child's IQ skills have been taken into account.

Working memory in the classroom

We often have to hold information in mind whilst engaged in an effortful activity. The information to be remembered may, for example, be the sentence that they intend to write while trying to spell the individual words. It could also be the list of instructions given by the teacher while carrying out individual steps in the task.

Individuals with small working memory capacity will struggle in these activities, simply because they are unable to hold in mind sufficient information to allow them to complete the task. Losing crucial information from working memory will cause them to forget many things: instructions they are attempting to follow; the details of what they are doing; where they have got to in a complicated task; and so on. Because those with small working memory capacity fail in many different activities on many occasions due to these kinds of forgetting, they will struggle to achieve normal rates of learning and so typically will make poor general academic progress.

Features of working memory failure

In order to understand in greater detail how working memory difficulties impact classroom performance, we observed children with normal IQ but low working memory skills during literacy and numeracy lessons. Working memory problems often go undetected in children and cannot be identified unequivocally without proper testing. However, here are some characteristics that are warning signs of poor working memory. The children typically:
• are well-adjusted socially
• are reserved in group activities in the classroom, rarely volunteering answers and sometimes not answering direct questions
• have short attention spans and high levels of distractibility, often forgetting part or all of instructions or messages
• fail to adequately monitor the quality of their work, and show a lack of creativity in solving complex problems
• frequently lose their place in complicated tasks which they may eventually abandon
• forget the content of messages and instructions
• are rated by their teachers at school entry as having relatively poor skills in areas such as reading, language, and mathematics
• show poor academic progress, particularly in literacy and mathematics
• have low levels of attainments at English, mathematics and science.

Purpose of the WMRS

Research has established that working memory capacity is closely associated with children's learning progress in the key academic domains of reading, maths, and science, across the full span of the school years. On this basis, assessing working memory at a very early stage in children's school careers provides a valuable means of identifying those individuals who are at risk of poor learning progress over subsequent years of school. This would provide the opportunity for prompt and early intervention that would minimise the adverse consequences of poor working memory capacity on academic learning. As the differences between typically developing children and those that are making relatively poor progress generally increase with age, the potential gains of effective early intervention could be very significant.

Given the impact of working memory deficits on the individual's ability to acquire knowledge, develop crucial skills and benefit from formal education, the identification of working memory impairments is a priority for many working with children with learning disabilities. The WMRS consists of 20 short descriptions of problem behaviours that differentiate children with low and average working memory abilities. The teacher rates how typical each behaviour is of the child on a scale ranging from *not typical at all* (0) to *very typical* (3). The behaviours are described in statements such as: i) *Does not volunteer answers in group situations*; ii) *To move on to the next step in an activity, needs frequent prompts by teaching staff*; and iii) *Mixes up material inappropriately, e.g. incorrectly combines parts from two sentences rather than reading each one accurately*. It is particularly valuable for teachers who do not wish to use more formal assessments of working memory, but do want to provide a more systematic evaluation of the potential working memory problems than can be provided by observation alone.

The WMRS has a number of merits. It takes no longer than five minutes to complete and is easy to score and interpret, requiring no psychometric training. It is valuable not only as a diagnostic screening tool for identifying children at risk of poor working memory, but also in illustrating both the classroom situations in which working memory failures frequently arise, and the profile of difficulties typically faced by children with low working memory. The rating scale will also enable teachers to use their informal knowledge of the child to produce an indicator of how likely it is that the child has a working memory problem. It provides a valuable first step in detecting possible working memory failures. Identification can then be followed up by examination of the individual's detailed profile of working memory strengths and weaknesses using standardised measures, such as the AWMA.

Chapter 2: Administering and scoring the WMRS

General testing considerations

Professional requirements

The WMRS is designed to be completed by any adult who has had extended contact with the child in a classroom setting. Typically this will be a teacher, but teaching assistants and teaching aides can also complete the WMRS. No formal training is required. In order to provide ratings that accurately reflect the child's behaviour, it is important that the individual has had a considerable amount of contact with the child, such as at least a month of regular contact.

Testing environment

The testing environment should be a quiet area. Ideally, the WMRS should be completed in one sitting. Once the Record Form has been completed, review it for blanks or multiple responses. If any are found, go back and respond to the skipped items or clarify any multiple responses.

Administration time

The WMRS will take approximately 5-10 minutes to complete.

Completing the WMRS

Go through each question on the Record Form and rate each of the 20 items by circling your chosen rating. The adult should rate each question on a four-point scale, ranging from 0 to 3. The rating choices are:

0   Not typical at all
1   Occasionally
2   Fairly typical
3   Very typical

Scoring the WMRS

Once all items have been completed, calculate the total score for the rater's responses. Transfer this sum to the box at the bottom of the page. Higher scores indicate greater impairments of working memory.

Missing responses

Check the Record Form for unanswered items. It is recommended that the total score is not calculated unless all items are appropriately scored.

Converting raw scores to *T* scores

The raw scores are converted into *T* scores. *T* scores are a way of describing an individual's performance with respect to the performance of others in the same age band. For example, if you are testing a child aged 5 years and 4 months, his/her performance will be compared with other children aged between 5:0 and 6:11 years. Average performance is indicated by a standard score of 50 and a standard deviation of 10.

Also available is the percentile for the total WMRS score. Percentiles represent the percentage of individuals in the same age band who obtained this score or less. The range of numbers falls between 1 and 100, with average performance represented by a percentile of 50.

To obtain a *T* score and percentile, look up the appropriate age range on the normative table provided in Appendix A. Higher scores reflect more problematic behaviour in the classroom and are associated with difficulties in working memory. The normative table is colour-coded to assist in the interpretation of the results. Scores in the Green range reflect classroom behaviours that are typical for a particular age group. Scores in the Amber range represents ratings that are one standard deviation above the mean (*T* score > 60) and are viewed as moderate working memory deficits. Scores in the Red range represents ratings that are two standard deviations above the mean (*T* score > 70) and are indicative of marked working memory impairments.

Chapter 3: Interpreting the WMRS

The WMRS provides a valuable first step in detecting possible working memory failures. This chapter describes how to interpret the WMRS score and how to effectively support a child's working memory skills in daily classroom activities.

Using the look-up table in Appendix A

Scores in the Green range

If a child's score falls in this range, it is unlikely that they have a working memory impairment. Continue to support and encourage their learning in the classroom.

Scores in the Amber range

If a child's score falls in this range, it is possible that they have a working memory impairment. It is recommended that the AWMA be administered in order to provide a detailed profile of their working memory strengths and weaknesses.

Scores in the Red range

If a child's score falls in this range, it is very likely that they have a working memory impairment. It is recommended that the AWMA be administered in order to confirm the nature and severity of this deficit. This individual has been identified as being at risk of poor educational progress over the coming years.

Supporting children with working memory problems

Children with a small working memory capacity often struggle in classroom activities, simply because they are unable to hold in mind sufficient information to allow them to complete a task. Losing crucial information from working memory will cause them to forget many things: instructions they are attempting to follow; the details of what they are doing; where they have got to in a complicated task; and so on. It is suggested that because children with low working memory often fail to meet the working memory demands of individual learning episodes, the incremental process of acquiring skill and knowledge over the school years is disrupted.

In order to effectively support a child's working memory in the classroom, it is important to recognise different classroom activities that involve working memory. Here are some examples.

Classroom activities that involve verbal working memory

- Remembering sequences of three or more numbers or unrelated words, such as *5, 9, 2, 6*, or *cat, lion, kangaroo*, or even unfamiliar letter combinations such as *'sp'* in Case Study 1.
- Remembering and successfully following lengthy instructions. Here is an example from a classroom of 6 and 7 year olds: *Put your sheets on the green table, arrow cards in the packet, put your pencil away, and come and sit on the carpet*. Often what happens is that children are able to perform the first part of the instruction and place their sheets on the green table and they are the first to sit down on the carpet. But they have forgotten the intermediate instructions and so have not done them. Even older children can have difficulty recalling instructions, as illustrated in Case Study 2.
- Remembering lengthy sentences containing some arbitrary content to be written down (e.g. *The speeding spider spied a spade* in the example with John in Case Study 1). If the sentence contains information that is not familiar to the child, they are more likely to forget it.
- Remembering sentences with complicated grammatical structure, such as *To blow up parliament, Guy Fawkes had 36 barrels of gunpowder.* It would help the child remember the sentence better if it were rephrased as *Guy Fawkes had 36 barrels of gunpowder* **to blow up parliament.**
- Identify digits on the 100 square/number line that follow a specific number pattern, e.g. odd/even numbers; multiples of 6; factors of 10, and so on.
- Identify the missing numbers in a sequence: *0, 1, 2, __, 4, 5, __.*
- Play *'Buzz'* to reinforce multiplication facts. Pupils all stand up and count in consecutive numbers from 1. If, for example, the game is focusing on multiples of three, pupils must say *'buzz'* if their number is a multiple of three when it is their turn (*1, 2, buzz, 4, 5, buzz, etc*). Pupils sit down when they respond incorrectly.

Classroom activities that involve visuo-spatial working memory

- Keeping track of the place reached in the course of multi-level tasks such as writing a sentence down either from memory or from the white board. Often what can happen is that a child can repeat or skip letters and words during sentence writing, or even miss out large chunks of a task.

- Using pictures or images to recall a story. They may get confused about the order of events in the story or even omit key events despite having a visual reminder.
- Retelling in chronological order a sequence of events from memory, using vocabulary words such as *first, second, next, last.*
- Remembering and performing rehearsed actions to lines of poetry.

What can be done to minimise the learning difficulties resulting from working memory impairments? One approach is to use effective classroom management to minimise memory-related failures in classroom-based learning activities. The following case studies illustrate both difficulties experienced by children with poor working memory skills (both had scored in the Red range in the WMRS) and useful strategies that a teacher can implement to support them.

Case Study 1

Oliver is a 5-year-old boy with an impairment of working memory. His nonverbal IQ and literacy and numeracy skills are below average and he is in the lowest ability groups in both literacy and numeracy, working for the majority of time at foundation level. The groups comprise of only 10 pupils in each and are both supported by a teaching assistant, with the extra support of an adult helper in literacy.

Learning activities are developed as far as possible to increase the meaningfulness and degree of familiarity of the material remembered to support Oliver and his peers. In literacy, for example, the main activity was to learn and use vocabulary correctly to indicate chronological order (*first, second, next, last, etc*). All teaching and learning involved in this activity was based on a recent class trip. The teacher showed several photos of various events that had taken place throughout the trip to remind the children as they shared their memories with one another. Though Oliver seemed to be fairly reserved and had participated very little in the lesson up to this point, he did become more involved in the class discussion about the photographs.

Frequent use and repetition of relevant task-specific vocabulary and information is another vital strategy for supporting children with impairment of working memory. In Oliver's literacy lesson, for example, the teacher frequently emphasised key words (*first, second, next, last, etc*) when encouraging the children to place the events in the photographs in chronological order. Oliver also benefited from other strategies employed by the teacher and teaching assistant to reduce working memory loads. For example, verbal and written information was always provided in the most simplified form and each step of the learning activities were modelled by the teacher as the pupils followed her. In addition, task instructions were broken down into key steps, allowing time for the pupils to perform each stage before moving onto the next point. For instance, the following instructions were carefully given to direct the children when giving out their individual whiteboards: *'Take a whiteboard then pass it on… Take a pen then pass the bag on… Put the pen on your board… Put the rubber on the board… Now you are ready to listen.'* However, despite re-structuring this multi-step task into separate independent steps, Oliver still lost his place in the task and didn't pass on the whiteboards as instructed.

On another occasion towards the end of the lesson, Oliver again lost his place in the task when asked to complete the sentence, *'Next, we will line up to…'* The teacher repeated the sentence, offering many clues about what was about to take place after the lesson. Oliver eventually replied, saying *'Next we will line up to go to the toy museum.'* Though the sentence made sense, Oliver hadn't moved on with the change in subject from the class trip to thinking about going for school dinner as the concurrent processing task had increased the working memory demands, thus leading to memory failure.

Case Study 2
Ellen is a 10-year-old girl with an impairment of working memory. Her nonverbal IQ and literacy and numeracy skills are below average and she is in the lowest ability groups in both literacy and numeracy. Ellen was observed in a numeracy lesson in which there were 10 pupils of relatively similar ability who were split into two groups.

The lesson began with the children sitting at their tables for the mental maths session in which the class played *'What number am I?'* The teacher reminded the children how to play the game as she encouraged them to ask focused questions about the number she was thinking of. She modelled examples of questions that could be asked to help the children work out her number, e.g. *'Is the number less than 20?'* and emphasised the use of specific mathematical vocabulary before giving volunteers the opportunity to lead the game.

Ellen participated well when asking questions about other pupils' numbers, though she did ask the same type of question each time which was based on an example that had been modelled by the teacher, e.g. *'If I partition it, will it be 30 and 3? Does it partition into 20 and 4? Does it partition into 70 and 2?'* She was also keen to take the leading role part-way through the game. However, as soon as the other pupils began to ask questions about her number, she quickly lost her enthusiasm to participate. When asked, *'Does the number have eight tens?'* Ellen did not respond. The teacher repeated the question and reminded her to think of the place value of her number, giving the prompts *'Does your number have tens? Do you know how many tens there are?'* Ellen was evidently struggling to hold the number in mind whilst attempting to answer questions about it and eventually told the teacher that she had forgotten it. At this point, the teacher spent a few minutes revising the concept of place value. She referred the children to the 100 square and the place value chart as she asked key questions such as *'How many tens does a number in the eighties have?'* and *'If a number has six tens, which row do we to point to on the 100 square?'* Ellen successfully answered this question, making good use of the visual aids available.

Moving onto the main part of the lesson, the pupils were reminded of the work completed the previous day which concentrated on thinking about *'one more/less than; 10 more/less than and 100 more/less than'*. The class worked together to review and mark the previous day's calculations as individuals volunteered to demonstrate on the whiteboard, e.g. *'10 more than 482 is 492'*. Ellen correctly answered a question directed at her, knowing that *'10 more than 382 is 392'*.

As this took place, the teacher constantly repeated crucial information such as the key vocabulary (*more than/less than*) and asked target questions to help the children gain greater understanding of the concepts being taught, e.g. *'If we are working out 10 more/less than a number, which part of the number changes?'* She often directed such questions towards Ellen to support her thinking processes. For instance, *'When thinking about 10 less than 307, Ellen, which part of the number will stay the same?'*

Ellen correctly stated, *'7'*.

'Which part of the number will change?'

Ellen replied, *'The 30. It gives 29.'*

Throughout this activity, the teacher did all she could to reduce the working memory load for Ellen and frequently evaluated the working demands of the task, gradually increasing the level from calculating 10 more/less than an number to 100 more/less than a number then extending this to working across the boundaries, e.g. *'What is 10 more than 99/197?'* She highlighted the pattern in the numbers when adding over the boundaries, i.e. *'The number moves to the next hundred,'* whilst studying many examples with the children. Ellen, however, left the classroom for a few minutes to collect her inhaler and evidently seemed to struggle to follow the work on her return. She began to fidget with her inhaler and didn't participate at all in the whole class discussion about the pattern in numbers.

As this main part of the lesson developed, Ellen became increasingly more distracted and appeared to lose total concentration. She began to swing on her chair, talk to her neighbour and shout out random comments unrelated to the task. The teacher reminded Ellen on several occasions to follow the usual classroom routines and actually stopped the class at one point to reinforce her expectations of behaviour: *'Stop talking. Put your pens down. Listen to me when I'm talking and put your hand up if you have something to say.'*

These instructions were clearly broken down by the teacher as she simultaneously pointed to the classroom rules displayed on the wall, thus allowing the children time to store and process the information.

Further details about the intervention programme can be found in the booklet *Understanding Working Memory: A Classroom Guide*, also published by Pearson Assessment.

Background information for educators on working memory can be found on our website: **www.york.ac.uk/res/wml/indexteachers.htm**. This is updated regularly and lists a series of publications that can be downloaded free of charge.

Chapter 4: Test development and standardisation

Test development

A starting point in developing the items in the WMRS was an observational study of children with low working memory but typical scores in IQ measures. Compared with classmates with typical working memory skills, the low-memory children frequently forgot instructions, struggled to cope with tasks involving simultaneous processing and storage and lost track of their place in complex tasks. The most common consequence of these failures was that the children abandoned the activity without completing it.

To increase the content validity of the WMRS, the majority of the individual items were based on additional group observations conducted by one of the authors (Hannah J. Kirkwood), who is an experienced classroom teacher. The observations were conducted in mainstream primary classrooms in demographically diverse areas that included children with both low and average working memory skills. Observation notes were reviewed in order to highlight frequently observed behaviours that corresponded to working memory deficits. Some examples include: 'The child raised his hand but when called upon, he had forgotten his response'; 'She lost her place in a task with multiple steps'; and 'The child has difficulty remaining on task'.

In order to refine the items that would be most useful in characterising children with working memory problems, interviews focusing on the child's behaviour in both structured learning and social contexts were conducted with the class teachers of 50 primary-age children with working memory deficits, selected randomly from a larger sample identified via routine screening. Each teacher also participated in a parallel interview based on a control child of the same sex, selected from the same class and with working memory standard scores in the average range (95-115). On the basis of these interviews, redundant items were eliminated and extra items added to more accurately represent descriptions of common classroom behaviours that discriminated children with low and normal working memory skills. The final version of the WMRS consisted of 20 items. Classroom teachers rated how typical each behaviour was of the children on a four-point frequency scale ranging from *not typical at all* (0) to *very typical* (3).

Normative sample

Demographic information

All individuals in the standardisation had English as their first language. The data collected for the norms include an equivalent proportion of males and females, and reflect a range of ethnic diversity in the UK, including those from African and Asian backgrounds. Neither sex nor ethnicity leads to significant differences in test performance. The number of males and females as a function of age is illustrated in Table 4.1.

A total of 417 children from primary schools in England participated in the study. Participating schools were selected to provide a nationally representative demographic sample on the basis of the national average of performance on national assessments in English, mathematics, and science that pupils sit in the final year of primary school at the age of 10 or 11. Schools in England are ranked on the basis of a combined or 'aggregate' score achieved in the three tests – the maximum possible being 300 (published by the Department for Education and Skills, 2006). Schools selected for the normative sample represent a range of low, average, and high performance in the combined score of the national test results. Schools were located in both urban and rural settings.

Table 4.1. *The number of males and females in the full sample as a function of age*

Age band	Total	Female	Male	Mean age (years:months)	Standard deviation (in months)
5-6	103	54	49	6:2	6.18
7-8	114	59	55	8:0	6.84
9	92	49	43	9:6	3.54
10-11	108	46	62	10:7	4.10

Reliability and validity

Test intercorrelations

The intercorrelations between the different memory tests are shown in Table 4.2. The coefficients indicate a strong relationship between all questions, supporting convergent validity. It is worth noting that these coefficients were not inflated by the large age variation in the sample.

Table 4.2. *The correlation coefficients between all measures of the WMRS (n = 417)*

	Q1	Q2	Q3	Q4	Q5	Q6	Q7	Q8	Q9	Q10	Q11	Q12	Q13	Q14	Q15	Q16	Q17	Q18	Q19	Q20
Q1	1.00																			
Q2	.67	1.00																		
Q3	.71	.60	1.00																	
Q4	.74	.63	.63	1.00																
Q5	.67	.59	.48	.62	1.00															
Q6	.70	.68	.59	.65	.66	1.00														
Q7	.81	.64	.65	.74	.67	.75	1.00													
Q8	.81	.65	.71	.74	.64	.75	.84	1.00												
Q9	.78	.68	.68	.68	.68	.76	.79	.81	1.00											
Q10	.52	.42	.44	.44	.37	.46	.48	.53	.54	1.00										
Q11	.73	.63	.68	.63	.64	.71	.71	.77	.79	.53	1.00									
Q12	.78	.65	.67	.67	.64	.73	.79	.82	.83	.53	.82	1.00								
Q13	.64	.61	.54	.59	.62	.76	.68	.69	.73	.45	.71	.76	1.00							
Q14	.68	.60	.55	.67	.62	.71	.70	.71	.72	.43	.66	.72	.72	1.00						
Q15	.60	.71	.59	.67	.56	.66	.61	.64	.64	.37	.64	.64	.65	.66	1.00					
Q16	.72	.64	.62	.62	.66	.77	.73	.77	.77	.48	.82	.78	.74	.68	.67	1.00				
Q17	.74	.68	.60	.67	.71	.75	.73	.74	.81	.43	.75	.74	.73	.74	.69	.79	1.00			
Q18	.74	.59	.59	.73	.65	.73	.76	.73	.72	.45	.67	.69	.68	.76	.66	.70	.74	1.00		
Q19	.80	.64	.67	.70	.67	.75	.79	.83	.82	.53	.81	.82	.73	.73	.70	.81	.77	.81	1.00	
Q20	.73	.65	.64	.67	.68	.77	.75	.77	.76	.47	.73	.79	.71	.69	.68	.75	.73	.74	.81	1.00

Note: All correlation coefficients are significant at the .01 level

Split-test reliability

Split-test reliability refers to the consistency with which a test can accurately measure what it aims to do. If an individual's performance remains consistent over repeated trials, it is considered to be reliable. Separate sums were calculated for the even-numbered and odd-numbered items across the whole sample. The correlation coefficient between these two total scores was .97, establishing internal reliability of the scale.

Construct validity

Construct validity refers to whether a test accurately measures the skills it is designed to measure. In order to evaluate whether the WMRS accurately identifies working memory deficits, correlations between the teacher ratings of 307 children and their composite scores in each of the four areas of memory tested in the AWMA were computed. The correlation coefficients are shown in Table 4.3. The total WMRS score was negatively correlated with composite recall scores of all four memory components as well as the processing scores for the working memory tasks (rs ranged from -.33 to -.43). This indicates that higher (i.e. more problematic) teacher ratings on the WMRS are associated with lower memory scores on the AWMA.

Table 4.3. *The correlation coefficients for test-retest reliability of the AWMA (n = 307)*

AWMA tests	WMRS total score
Verbal short-term memory	-.34
Verbal working memory: recall	-.43
Verbal working memory: processing	-.42
Visuo-spatial short-term memory	-.36
Visuo-spatial working memory: recall	-.35
Visuo-spatial working memory: processing	-.33

Diagnostic validity

The WMRS is the first standardised rating scale for non-specialist assessors, such as classroom teachers, to screen their pupils for significant working memory problems quickly and effectively. In order to evaluate the extent to which the WMRS is able to identify children who will struggle in key areas of their learning, we compared ratings of the WMRS with two verbal working memory tests from the AWMA and the *Wechsler Intelligence Scale for Children – Fourth UK Edition* (WISC-IV^UK) Working Memory Index

(WMI) (Weschler, 2004) in children with low and average working memory skills. The WMI is comprised of three verbal memory tasks: a forward and backward digit span and a letter-number sequencing task. The forward and backward digit span tasks correspond closely to those in the AWMA. In the letter-number sequencing task, the child is presented with a mixture of numbers and letters and has to repeat the numbers first in ascending order followed by the letters in alphabetical order.

We evaluated the efficacy of using the WMRS to reliably identify individuals with working memory problems. In order to do this, two groups of children were selected via routine screening. The first group comprised of 45 children with poor working memory (i.e. composite scores at or below the 10th centile in Listening Recall and Backward Digit Recall of the AWMA): a young group consisting of 15 boys and 10 girls, with a mean age of 5 years 8 months (SD = 4.11 months, range = 5:1 to 6:3 years), and an older group consisting of 15 boys and 5 girls, with a mean age of 9 years 9 months (SD = 3.1 months, range = 9:4 to 10:2 years). None of the children were diagnosed with physical or sensory impairments. The second group was an age-matched sample of 46 children with average working memory (mean standard scores of 96 and 105 for Listening Recall and Backward Digit Recall, respectively). These children were selected from the same school and classes as the low working memory children. The younger group consisted of 9 boys and 16 girls, with a mean age of 6 years 3 months (SD = 2.97, range = 71 to 81 months). The older group consisted of 11 boys and 10 girls, with a mean age of 10 years 4 months (SD = 4.1, range = 118 to 130 months). All participants in both groups were native English speakers.

Descriptive statistics for the standard scores of the two AWMA screening measures and scaled scores for the tests of the WISC-IV[UK] WMI as a function of working memory skills are shown in Table 4.4. For the WMRS, the T score (with a population mean of 50 and SD of 10) is shown for the total score. The group mean on the WMRS confirms that the low working memory children performed at a level of risk (i.e. one standard deviation above the mean of 50) compared to the average working memory children. Correspondingly, mean scores for the WISC-IV[UK] WMI were markedly higher for the average working memory group compared to the low working memory group. This establishes a high degree of convergence between the direct assessment of working memory using the AWMA and WISC-IV[UK] WMI and the behaviour ratings from the WMRS.

Table 4.4. *Descriptive statistics for the WMRS, AWMA and WISC-IV^UK WMI as a function of working memory skills*

Measure	Low working memory (n = 45)		Average working memory (n = 46)	
	Mean	SD	Mean	SD
AWMA: Listening Recall	74.09	4.40	96.30	10.24
AWMA: Backward Digit Recall	75.93	6.77	105.50	9.94
WMRS Total*	64.24	11.16	46.22	7.83
	Low working memory (n = 27)		Average working memory (n = 38)	
WISC-IV^UK WMI Digit Span**	5.93	2.34	11.05	2.31
Letter-Number Sequencing**	5.89	2.03	6.63	3.08
WMI	76.41	7.57	92.79	12.55

* T score = mean of 50 and standard deviation of 10
** Scaled scores = mean of 10 and standard deviation of 3

We also investigated how well the WMRS teacher ratings differentiated the low and average working memory groups. In total, 76% of children with poor working memory and 80% of the average working memory children were correctly identified. This establishes that the WMRS is effective at discriminating children in the two working memory groups, with higher scores typically characterising children with working memory deficits.

Recent publications by the authors

Our research findings on the relationship between working memory and learning are also published widely in both professional journals and peer-reviewed academic journals.

Professional journals

Alloway, T.P. (2006). Making 'working memory' work in the classroom. *Early Years Update*, *42*, 9-11.

Alloway, T.P. & Gathercole, S.E. (2005). How working memory can impact learning in the classroom. *Teaching, Thinking & Creativity Magazine, 18*, 48-51.

Alloway, T.P. & Temple, K.J. (2005). A comparison of working memory profiles of children with Developmental Coordination Disorder and Moderate Learning Difficulties. *Dyspraxia Review, 4*, 29-42.

Gathercole, S.E, & Alloway, T.P. (2004). Working memory and classroom learning. *Dyslexia Review, 15*, 4-9.

Gathercole, S.E, & Alloway, T.P. (2004). Working memory and classroom learning. *Professional Association for Teachers of Students with Specific Learning Difficulties, 17*, 2-12.

Books

Alloway, T.P. & Gathercole, S.E. (2006, Editors). *Working memory and neurodevelopmental conditions*. Hove: Psychology Press.

Gathercole, S.E. & Alloway, T.P. (2008). *Working memory and learning: A practical guide.* Sage Publications.

Gathercole, S.E. & Alloway, T.P. (2005). *Understanding working memory: A classroom guide.* London: Pearson Assessment.

Academic journals
Theoretical development of working memory
Alloway, T.P. & Gathercole, S.E. (2005). Working memory and short-term sentence recall in young children. *European Journal of Cognitive Psychology, 17*, 207-220.

Alloway, T.P., Gathercole, S.E, Kirkwood, H.J., & Elliott, J.E. (in press). Evaluating the validity of the Automated Working Memory Assessment. *Educational Psychology*.

Alloway, T.P., Gathercole, S.E., & Pickering, S.J. (2006). Verbal and visuo-spatial short-term and working memory in children: Are they separable? *Child Development, 77*, 1698-1716.

Alloway, T.P., Gathercole, S.E., Willis, C., & Adams, A.M. (2004). A structural analysis of working memory and related cognitive skills in early childhood. *Journal of Experimental Child Psychology, 87*, 85-106.

Alloway, T.P., Willis, C., & Wylie, J. (2007). Developmental changes in working memory: From childhood to adulthood. *Manuscript submitted for publication.*

Conlin, J.A. & Gathercole, S.E. (2006). Lexicality and interference in working memory in children and adults. *Journal of Memory and Language, 55*, 363-380.

Conlin, J.A., Gathercole, S.E., & Adams, J.W. (2005). Stimulus similarity decrements in children's working memory span. *Quarterly Journal of Experimental Psychology, 58A*, 1434-1446.

Conlin, J.A., Gathercole, S.E., & Adams, J.W. (2005). Children's working memory: Investigating performance limitations in complex span tasks. *Journal of Experimental Child Psychology, 90*, 303-317.

Gathercole, S.E, & Alloway, T.P. (2006). Working memory deficits in neurodevelopmental disorders. *Journal of Child Psychology and Psychiatry, 47*, 4-15.

Lobley, K., Gathercole, S.E., & Baddeley, A.D. (2005). Phonological similarity effects in verbal complex span. *Quarterly Journal of Experimental Psychology, 58A*, 1462-1478.

St Clair-Thompson, H.L., & Gathercole, S.E. (2006). Executive functions and achievements on national curriculum tests: Shifting, updating, inhibition, and working memory. *Quarterly Journal of Experimental Psychology, 59, 746-759.*

Working memory and learning

Alloway, T.P. (in press). Working memory, but not IQ, predicts subsequent learning in children with learning difficulties. *European Journal of Psychological Assessment.*

Alloway, T.P. & Gathercole, S.E. (2006). How does working memory work in the classroom? *Educational Research and Reviews, 1,* 134-139.

Alloway, T.P., Gathercole, S.E., Adams, A.M., & Willis, C., Eaglen, R., & Lamont, E. (2005). Working memory and other cognitive skills as predictors of progress towards early learning goals at school entry. *British Journal of Developmental Psychology, 23*, 417-426.

Alloway, T.P., Gathercole, S.E., Kirkwood, H., & Elliott, J. (2007). The cognitive and behavioural characteristics of children with low working memory. *Manuscript submitted for publication.*

Alloway, T.P., Gathercole, S.E., Willis, C., & Adams, A.M. (2005). Working memory and special educational needs. *Educational and Child Psychology, 22,* 56-67.

Alloway, T.P. & Gathercole, S.E. (2005). The role of sentence recall in reading and language skills of children with learning difficulties. *Learning and Individual Differences, 15,* 271-282.

Gathercole, S.E. (2006). Nonword repetition and word learning: The nature of the relationship. *Applied Psycholinguistics, 27,* 513-543.

Gathercole, S.E. (2006). Complexities and constraints in nonword repetition and word learning. *Applied Psycholinguistics, 27,* 599-613.

Gathercole, S.E. (2004). Working memory and learning during the school years. *Proceedings of the British Academy, 125,* 365-380.

Gathercole, S.E, Alloway, T.P., Kirkwood, H.J., & Elliott, J.E. (in press). Attentional and executive function behaviours in children with poor working memory. *Learning & Individual Differences.*

Gathercole, S.E., Alloway, T.P., Willis, C., & Adams, A.M. (2006). Working memory in children with reading disabilities. *Journal of Experimental Child Psychology, 93,* 265-281.

Gathercole, S.E., Brown, L., & Pickering, S.J. (2003). Working memory assessments at school entry as longitudinal predictors of National Curriculum attainment levels. *Educational and Child Psychology, 20,* 109-122.

Gathercole, S.E., Pickering, S.J., Ambridge, B., & Wearing, H. (2004). The structure of working memory from 4 to 15 years of age. *Developmental Psychology, 40,* 177-190.

Gathercole, S.E., Pickering, S.J., Knight, C., & Stegmann, Z. (2004). Working memory skills and educational attainment: Evidence from National Curriculum assessments at 7 and 14 years of age. *Applied Cognitive Psychology, 40,* 1-16.

Jarvis, H.L., & Gathercole, S.E. (2003). Verbal and non-verbal working memory and achievements on national curriculum tests at 11 and 14 years of age. *Educational and Child Psychology, 20,* 123-140.

Masoura, E.V., & Gathercole, S.E. (2005). Phonological short-term memory skills and new word learning in young Greek children. *Memory, 13,* 422-429.

Alloway, T.P. (2007). Working Memory, Reading and Mathematical Skills in Children with Developmental Coordination Disorder. *Journal of Experimental Child Psychology, 96,* 20-36.

Alloway, T.P., & Archibald, L.M. (in press). Working Memory and Learning in Children with Developmental Coordination Disorder and Specific Language Impairment. *Journal of Learning Disabilities.*

Alloway, T.P., Gathercole, S.E. (2005). The role of sentence recall in reading and language skills of children with learning difficulties. *Learning and Individual Differences. 15,* 271-282.

Alloway, T.P., Rajendran, G., Archibald, L.M., & Pickering, S. (2007). Working memory profiles of atypical children. *Manuscript submitted for publication.*

Alloway, T.P. & Temple, K.J. (2007). A Comparison of Working Memory Profiles and Learning in Children with Developmental Coordination Disorder and Moderate Learning Difficulties. *Applied Cognitive Psychology, 21,* 473-487.

Alloway, T.P., & Warner, C. (in press). The Effect of Task-Specific Training on Learning and Memory in Children with Developmental Coordination Disorder. *Perceptual and motor skills.*

Archibald, L.M., & Alloway, T.P. (in press). Comparing Language Profiles: Children with Specific Language Impairment and Developmental Coordination Disorder. *International Journal of Communication and Language Disorders.*

Archibald, L.M., & Gathercole, S.E. (2007). Nonword repetition in Specific Language Impairment: more than a phonological short-term memory deficit. *Psychonomic Bulletin & Review, 14,* 919-924.

Archibald, L.M., & Gathercole, S.E. (2007). Nonword repetition and serial recall: Equivalent measures of verbal short-term memory? *Applied Psycholinguistics, 28,* 587-606.

Archibald, L.M., & Gathercole, S.E. (2007). The complexities of complex span: Storage and processing deficits in Specific Language Impairment. *Journal of Memory and Language, 57,* 177-194.

Archibald, L.M., & Gathercole, S. E. (2006). Short-term and working memory in Specific Language Impairment. *International Journal of Communication Disorders, 41.* 675-693.

Archibald, L.M., & Gathercole, S.E. (2006). Nonword repetition: A comparison of tests. *Journal of Speech, Language, and Hearing Research*, *49*, 970-983.

Briscoe, J., Gathercole, S.E., & Marlow, N. (2001). Everyday memory and cognitive ability in children born very prematurely. *Journal of Child Psychology and Psychiatry, 42,* 749-754.

Gathercole, S.E., (2008). Deficits in verbal long-term memory and learning in children with poor phonological short-term memory skills. *Quarterly Journal of Experimental Psychology*, *61*, 474-490.

Gathercole, S.E., Alloway, T.P., Kirkwood, H.J., Elliott, J.G., Holmes, J., & Hilton, K.A. (in press). Attentional and executive behavioural profiles of children with poor working memory. *Learning and Individual Differences*.

Gathercole, S.E., Durling, M., Evans, S., Jeffcock, & S. Stone (in press). Working memory abilities and children's performance in laboratory analogues of classroom activities. *Applied Cognitive Psychology*.

Gathercole, S.E., Tiffany, C., Briscoe, J., Thorn, A.S.C., & ALSPAC Team (2005). Developmental consequences of poor phonological short-term memory function in childhood: A longitudinal study. *Journal of Child Psychology and Psychiatry*. *46*, 598-611.

Keehner, M., & Gathercole, S.E. (2007). Cognitive adaptations arising from non-native experience of sign language in hearing adults. *Memory and Cognition*, *35*, 752-761.

Pickering, S. J. & Gathercole, S.E. (2004). Distinctive working memory profiles in children with special educational needs. *Educational Psychology*, *24,* 393-408.

Spooner, A., Gathercole, S.E., & Baddeley, A.D. (2006). Does weak reading comprehension reflect an integration deficit? *Journal of Research in Reading*, *29,* 173-193.

Appendix A: *T* scores and percentiles

Total	Ages 5-6		Ages 7-8		Age 9		Ages 10-11	
	T score	Percentile	*T* score	Percentile	*T* score	Percentile	*T* score	Percentile
0	37	3	41	13	41	12	40	10
1	38	9	42	29	42	28	41	22
2	38	13	43	36	43	36	41	27
3	39	16	43	42	43	39	42	32
4	39	19	44	46	44	41	43	36
5	40	21	44	50	45	45	43	38
6	41	24	45	52	46	48	44	40
7	41	26	46	54	46	51	45	45
8	42	28	46	54	47	54	45	47
9	42	31	47	56	48	55	46	48
10	43	33	48	57	48	57	47	49
11	44	34	48	58	49	60	47	51
12	44	35	49	59	50	63	48	53
13	45	38	50	59	50	64	49	54
14	45	40	50	60	51	65	50	54
15	46	41	51	62	52	68	50	55
16	47	43	51	65	52	70	51	56
17	47	44	52	66	53	71	52	57
18	48	47	53	67	54	73	52	59
19	48	49	53	68	55	74	53	62
20	49	50	54	68	55	77	54	69
21	50	52	55	69	56	77	54	75
22	50	54	55	70	57	78	55	76
23	51	57	56	72	57	79	56	77
24	51	60	57	75	58	80	56	77
25	52	64	57	77	59	83	57	78
26	53	65	58	79	59	84	58	78
27	53	67	58	79	60	85	59	79
28	54	68	59	80	61	85	59	81
29	54	70	60	81	61	86	60	82
30	55	71	60	82	62	87	61	83

Appendix A: *continued*

Total	Ages 5-6		Ages 7-8		Age 9		Ages 10-11	
	T score	Percentile	*T* score	Percentile	*T* score	Percentile	*T* score	Percentile
31	56	71	61	82	63	88	61	84
32	56	72	62	84	63	88	62	84
33	57	74	62	85	64	89	63	84
34	58	76	63	86	65	89	63	85
35	58	77	63	87	66	90	64	87
36	59	78	64	88	66	90	65	88
37	59	79	65	89	67	90	65	89
38	60	80	65	90	68	91	66	89
39	61	82	66	91	68	92	67	91
40	61	83	67	93	69	92	68	92
41	62	86	67	94	70	93	68	95
42	62	89	68	94	70	95	69	97
43	63	90	69	94	71	96	70	98
44	64	90	69	95	72	97	70	98
45	64	92	70	95	72	97	71	98
46	65	92	70	95	73	97	72	98
47	65	93	71	95	74	97	72	99
48	66	93	72	96	75	97	73	99
49	67	94	72	97	75	98	74	99
50	67	94	73	98	76	98	74	99
51	68	95	74	99	77	98	75	99
52	68	95	74	99	77	98	76	99
53	69	95	75	99	78	99	77	99
54	70	96	75	99	79	99	77	99
55	70	96	76	99	79	99	78	99
56	71	96	77	99	80	99.9	79	99.9
57	71	97	77	99.9	80	99.9	79	99.9
58	72	97	78	99.9	80	99.9	80	99.9
59	73	98	79	99.9	80	99.9	81	99.9
60	73	99.9	79	99.9	80	99.9	81	99.9

Appendix B: Acknowledgements to participating schools

We gratefully acknowledge the support of the headteachers, special educational needs co-ordinators (SENCOs) and teachers at the following schools who volunteered to assist us in collecting norms for this test.

Blue Coat Church of England Junior School
Bowburn Infants and Junior School
Brandon Junior School
Bullion Lane Primary School
Burnopfield Primary School
Burnside Primary School
Coxhoe Primary School
Easington Colliery Primary School
Finchale Primary School
Gilesgate Primary School
Greenland Junior School
Kelloe Primary School
Langley Moor Primary School
Leadgate Community Junior School
Lumley Junior School
Newker Primary School
Pelton Community Primary School
Red Rose Primary School
Sacristan Junior School
St Godric's Roman Catholic Voluntary Aided Primary School
Tyneview Primary School
Wheatley Hill Community Primary School